Looking for Animals

By Will Stratford

Illustrated by David Sheldon

Target Skill Main Idea

Scott Foresman
is an imprint of

We look for animals
in the grass.

Tad sees a blue bird.

Val spots a nest.

We see the bird
on the nest.

A green bug jumps
on my leg!

A frog is on my hand.

I like to draw the duck.